Crisis Management

Strategies for Resilience and

Adaptation in Times of Uncertainty

Isaac Wilson

Table of Contents

Crisis Management

Introduction

Organizations are more susceptible to a variety of crises in today's fast-paced and connected world, which can impair operations, harm their reputation, and even endanger their existence. Emergencies can take many different forms, from cyberattacks and natural disasters to pandemics and financial downturns, and they can happen suddenly, leaving communities and businesses in ruins. We'll examine the idea of crisis management in this section, including what it means and why adaptability and resilience are so important during uncertain times.

Comprehending the Crisis Management Concept

The process of recognizing, anticipating, responding to, and recovering from emergencies or crises that endanger an organization's operations, stakeholders, or reputation is known as crisis management. It entails a concerted effort to lessen the effects of a crisis, protect the welfare of individuals impacted, minimize disruption, and aid in recovery.

Fundamentally, crisis management is about being ready for anything unexpected. Organizations must create proactive plans and strategies to deal with possible crises before they happen, as well as mobilize resources and respond skillfully when crises do inevitably strike.

Risk assessment, preparation planning, communication techniques, leadership and decision-making, resilience building, adaptation, recovery initiatives, and learning from previous experiences are some of the essential elements of crisis management.

Through the integration of these elements into an all-encompassing crisis management framework, organizations can augment their capacity to adeptly navigate unpredictable and turbulent milieus.

Importance of Adaptation and Resilience in Uncertain Times

Resilience and adaptability become critical in uncertain times for organizations hoping to weather the storm and come out stronger on the other side. While adaptation refers to the ability to flourish in changing circumstances, resilience is the capacity to withstand and recover from adversity.

Organizations that possess resilience are able to withstand shocks, recover from setbacks, and continue operations even in the face of disruption. It entails creating resilient structures, procedures, and systems that can tolerate difficulties and stressors in addition to encouraging a resilient mindset among stakeholders and staff.

Conversely, adaptation entails being nimble and adaptable in the face of changing circumstances and new threats. Organizations must welcome change, come up with creative solutions, and grab chances in the face of uncertainty. Organizations can set themselves up for success in challenging times by continuously surveying the horizon, spotting emerging trends, and making proactive adjustments to strategies and operations.

Resilience and adaptation are essential components of crisis management strategies for organizations because of the volatile and unpredictable nature of today's world, where crises can occur at any time and without warning. In the face of adversity, those who can successfully navigate uncertainty, foresee difficulties, and quickly adjust to changing circumstances will not only survive but also thrive.

To sum up, crisis management is an essential task for companies trying to successfully navigate unpredictable and turbulent environments.

Organizations can improve their capacity to endure crises, reduce disruption, and emerge stronger on the other side by comprehending the idea of crisis management, giving resilience and adaptation top priority, and putting proactive strategies and plans into action.

The necessity for resilience and adaptation, as well as the significance of crisis management, will only grow as the rate of change quickens and crises become more complex.

Chapter 1: Types of Crisis

Crises are unavoidable events that have the potential to seriously impair an organization's or community's regular operation. They can be caused by a wide range of things, from hostile assaults and human error to natural calamities and technology malfunctions. It is essential for good crisis management to comprehend the various kinds of crises that organizations could encounter. This section will examine the different kinds of crises and how they affect communities and businesses.

Exploring Different Types of Crisis

1. Natural Disasters: Natural processes can generate abrupt and catastrophic occurrences including earthquakes, hurricanes, floods, wildfires, and tsunamis. These emergencies may cause significant harm to the infrastructure, fatalities, population displacement, and interruptions of vital services.

To lessen the effects of natural disasters on their operations and to guarantee the security and well-being of their stakeholders and employees, organizations need to have strong strategies in place for both preparedness and response to catastrophes.

2. Technological Failures: Power outages, equipment malfunctions, data breaches, cyberattacks, and system failures are just a few examples of the many problems that fall under the category of technological failures. These emergencies may result in lost data, downtime, financial losses, harm to one's reputation, and fines from the authorities. For organizations to effectively prevent and address technical failures, they need to invest in strong IT infrastructure, cybersecurity measures, and backup plans.

3. Public Health Emergencies: Pandemics, infectious disease outbreaks, and bioterrorism attacks are examples of public health emergencies that provide serious difficulties for people and organizations around the globe. In addition to

jeopardizing the health and safety of staff members and clients, these crises have the potential to interrupt supply chains, operations, and customer demand. To lessen the effects of public health emergencies, organizations must put employee health and safety first, put infection control procedures in place, and modify how they conduct business.

4. Financial Crises: Financial crises can have a significant impact on communities and businesses. Examples of these include banking crises, stock market crashes, economic recessions, and currency crises. These crises may result in reduced consumer spending, market instability, bankruptcies, layoffs, and credit constraints. To weather financial crises and ensure

long-term survival, organizations need to diversify their revenue sources, implement sensible financial management procedures, and maintain solid liquidity levels.

5. Reputational Crisis: Scandals, controversies, bad press, and unethical actions that damage an organization's credibility and reputation can all lead to reputational crises.

These crises have the potential to reduce stakeholder trust, harm brand equity, and cause employers, investors, and customers to leave. To repair trust and restore confidence in their brand, organizations need to take proactive measures to manage their reputation, communicate in a genuine and transparent manner, and act quickly to address any issues that arise.

Impact of Each Type of Crisis on Businesses and Communities

1. Operational Disruption: Crises can cause interruptions to regular business operations, which can result in lost productivity, downtime, and delays in the delivery of goods or services. Financial losses, lost opportunities, and strained client relations may arise from this.

2. Financial losses: For businesses, crises can have serious financial repercussions, such as lost revenue, higher expenses, and

property or asset damage. This can exacerbate economic instability and endanger an organization's sustainability and financial health.

3. Humans Impact: The health, safety, and well-being of workers, clients, and communities can all be impacted by crises. The significance of placing human welfare at the top of the priority list in crisis management activities is highlighted by the possibility of injuries, fatalities, psychological trauma, displacement, and loss of livelihood.

4. Reputational Damage: A crisis can undermine a company's credibility and reputation, which can lead to a decline in trust, bad press, and long-term harm to

brand equity. Rebuilding reputation and trust can be difficult and time-consuming processes that call for sincere attempts to solve underlying problems as well as proactive communication.

5. Community Resilience: Crises put a community's resiliency and cohesiveness to the test by uniting individuals to help one another, pool resources, and triumph over hardship. Effective crisis response and recovery depend on strong community partnerships and teamwork, which help communities recover and prosper after a disaster.

In conclusion, successful crisis management requires a grasp of the various kinds of crises that companies may encounter as well as how they affect communities and enterprises. Organizations are better equipped to withstand hardship and come out stronger when they anticipate possible crises, create thorough planning and reaction plans, and encourage resilience and adaptation. To maintain their long-term success and sustainability, organizations need to be alert and proactive in identifying and resolving new dangers as the pace of change quickens and the complexity of crises escalates.

Chapter 2: Risk Assessment and Preparedness

Effective crisis management requires both risk assessment and readiness. Organisations can reduce risks, improve resilience, and lessen the effect of crises when they arise by methodically identifying possible crises, assessing their likelihood and impact, and creating plans and strategies for preparation. We'll get into risk assessment and readiness in this section, looking at how businesses may recognise and get ready for any emergencies.

Identifying Potential Crises through Risk Assessments

1. Identifying Dangers: Finding possible risks or hazards that could cause a crisis is the first stage in performing a risk assessment. Natural disasters like hurricanes, floods, and earthquakes may fall under this category. Technological dangers include equipment malfunctions and power outages. Man-made dangers include terrorist attacks and accidents. Operational dangers include supply chain interruptions and financial problems.

2. Likelihood and Impact Assessment: Organizations need to evaluate the possibility and consequences of each

possible danger after it has been identified. To ascertain the likelihood of each danger materializing and the possible repercussions in the event that it does, this entails reviewing past data, performing scenario assessments, and conferring with subject matter experts.

3. Risk Prioritization: Organizations can rank risks based on the severity and urgency of each based on the likelihood and impact assessments. In addition to ensuring that less important risks are not ignored, this aids organizations in concentrating their resources and efforts on addressing the biggest and most pressing issues first.

4. Assessment of Vulnerability: Organizations need to analyze not only the

possibility and impact of risks, but also their susceptibility to each one. Finding weaknesses in current infrastructure, procedures, and systems that could make a crisis worse and make response and recovery more difficult is part of this approach.

5. Stakeholder Engagement: Employees, clients, suppliers, government organisations, and community members are just a few of the many stakeholders whose opinions should be considered during risk assessment. Incorporating stakeholders into the risk assessment procedure guarantees that a range of viewpoints are taken into account and that any hazards are found and investigated thoroughly.

Developing Preparedness Plans and Strategies

1. Establishment of Purpose and Goals: Clear objectives and goals must be established before creating any plans or tactics for readiness. These goals should represent the organization's dedication to safeguarding the interests, safety, and well-being of its stakeholders and be consistent with its mission and core values.

2. Identification of Duties and Responsibilities: Plans for preparedness should explicitly outline the roles and duties of important individuals and parties participating in crisis management. Identifying the people in charge of communication, resource allocation,

decision-making, and response effort coordination is part of this.

3. Development of Response Protocols: Specific protocols and procedures to be followed in the case of a crisis should be outlined in preparation. This covers procedures for deploying resources, coordinating with stakeholders, evaluating the situation, triggering the crisis management team, and carrying out reaction plans.

4. Training and Exercise : Organizations must undertake exercises and offer training to staff members to acquaint them with crisis response protocols and processes in order to guarantee preparedness and effectiveness. To measure reaction skills and

pinpoint areas for development, this may use tabletop exercises, simulations, drills, and scenario-based training sessions.

5. Technology Inclusion: In order for organizations to coordinate, communicate, and work together more successfully during times of crisis, technology is essential to crisis preparedness and response. Plans for preparedness should include digital platforms and tools for data sharing, communication, resource management, and situational awareness.

6. Continuous Improvement: Responses to developing threats, conditions, and learning from the past should be factored into dynamic and flexible preparedness strategies. To ensure that their readiness

plans remain successful and relevant over time, organisations should review and update them on a regular basis, taking into account user input, industry best practices, and new trends.

In conclusion, risk assessment and readiness are essential elements of a successful crisis management strategy. They help organisations recognise possible crises, estimate their likelihood and consequences, and create proactive plans and strategies to reduce risks and build resilience.

Organisations can mitigate the effects of crises and protect the safety, welfare, and interests of their stakeholders by carrying out detailed risk assessments, including stakeholders, and formulating comprehensive preparedness plans. Organisations need to be alert and proactive in recognising and mitigating emerging risks in order to secure their long-term viability and sustainability, particularly as the rate of change quickens and crisis complexity rises.

Chapter 3: Communication Strategies

Organizations must communicate effectively during crises in order to control the situation, uphold stakeholder trust, and lessen the crisis's effects. This section will discuss the value of efficient communication in times of crisis and provide tips for putting plans and procedures for crisis communication into practice.

Importance of Crisis Communication Effectiveness

1.   Preserving Credibility and Trust: Establishing and maintaining trust and credibility with employees, customers, investors, and the general public are all made possible by effective communication within firms. Clear and prompt communication shows a dedication to transparency and responsibility while also fostering trust in the organization's crisis management capabilities.

2.   Giving Accurate Information: Stakeholders look for accurate and trustworthy information during emergencies so they may comprehend the circumstances and make wise decisions. Good communication helps stop the spread of false information, rumors, and conjecture

by ensuring that stakeholders receive timely updates and pertinent information.

3. Managing Expectations: In times of crisis, communication plays a crucial role in controlling stakeholders' expectations about the organization's reaction, timetable for recovery, and possible effects. Organizations can assist stakeholders in understanding the difficulties and uncertainties related to the crisis and making appropriate preparations by setting clear and reasonable expectations.

4. Handling Emotions and Concerns: Stakeholders are frequently gripped by intense feelings and worries during crises, such as fear, anxiety, and uncertainty. Good communication recognizes and responds to these worries, giving individuals impacted

by the crisis comfort, compassion, and support.

5. Exhibiting Transparency and Leadership:
A company's ability to effectively communicate shows leadership and transparency, which gives stakeholders trust and promotes a feeling of cohesion and togetherness. Organizations can gain stakeholders' trust and credibility by being transparent with information sharing, owning up to mistakes, and accepting accountability for their actions.

Implementing Crisis Communication Plans and Protocols

1. Creating a Plan for Crisis Communication: A defined structure outlining the roles, duties, procedures, and protocols for communication during crises is known as a crisis communication plan. To guarantee a well-coordinated and efficient reaction, it identifies important players, communication routes, messaging tactics, and escalation protocols.

2. Creating Channels of Communication: Establishing several communication channels is crucial for organizations to efficiently reach diverse stakeholders. These channels could include direct communication (phone calls, meetings), digital media (websites, social media), traditional media (press releases, media

briefings), and internal communication channels (email, intranet).

3. Creating Messages That Are Clear and Consistent: In order to guarantee that stakeholders receive accurate and coherent information during emergencies, clear and consistent messaging is crucial. Communications about the issue should be succinct, truthful, sympathetic, and address important queries, worries, and updates.

4. Assigning Representatives: During times of crisis, organizations ought to assign spokespersons who have received training to deal with the media and interested parties. A spokeswoman should be able to react to queries and concerns from stakeholders

while also being informed, trustworthy, and sympathetic.

5. Monitoring and Organizing Communication: In order to rapidly handle misinformation, rumors, and growing difficulties during a crisis, companies need to actively monitor and manage communication channels. This could entail keeping an eye on public opinion, news coverage, and social media in addition to instantly answering questions and giving updates.

6. Continually Providing Updates: In order to keep stakeholders informed and involved during emergencies, regular updates are necessary. Updates on the situation's evolution, reaction activities, recovery

efforts, and any modifications to protocols or plans should be given by organizations on a timely basis. Updates ought to be honest, proactive, and catered to the varying needs and preferences of the many stakeholder groups.

7. Assessing and Modifying Communication Techniques: Organizations should thoroughly assess their communication tactics and results after the crisis has passed. This entails evaluating the efficacy of response methods, spokespersons, communication channels, and messaging in order to pinpoint areas that require improvement. To improve preparedness and resilience, future communication plans and processes should include lessons learnt from previous crises.

To sum up, efficient communication is essential for managing the issue, upholding stakeholder trust, and lessening the crisis' effects. Organizations may guarantee clear, prompt, and compassionate communication that attends to the needs and concerns of stakeholders by putting crisis communication plans and practices into place. Organizations must emphasize good communication as a fundamental element of their crisis management efforts as the pace of change quickens and the complexity of crises escalates in order to traverse uncertainty and come out stronger on the other side.

Chapter 4: Leadership and Decision Making

To effectively navigate through difficult times and ensure that organizations respond to crises, leadership and decision-making are essential components of crisis management. This section will look at how leadership functions in crisis situations and how decisions are made when things are unclear.

Role of Leadership in Crisis Management

1. Establishing the Tone: By establishing clear expectations, priorities, and values, effective leadership sets the standard for crisis management. To inspire confidence and trust among stakeholders and cultivate a sense of unity and purpose within the organization, leaders must exhibit composure, resilience, and confidence.

2. Giving Instruction: In times of crisis, leaders furnish guidance and direction to guarantee that the organization reacts to the circumstances efficiently. This entails establishing strategic goals, assigning funds, and deploying staff to handle urgent concerns and lessen the crisis' effects.

3. Making Difficult Choices: Leaders frequently have to make difficult choices in the face of uncertainty and pressure during crises. Decisions about how to allocate resources, manage risks, communicate with stakeholders, and set organizational priorities may fall under this category. In order to safeguard the interests of the organization and the welfare of its stakeholders, effective leaders must carefully consider the advantages and disadvantages of every choice they make.

4. Effective Communication: Effective communication is a fundamental leadership skill in crisis management, allowing leaders to inform, reassure, and instill trust in stakeholders. It is imperative for leaders to engage in transparent, authentic, and

empathetic communication to effectively address the concerns of stakeholders and keep them updated on decisions, actions, and developments.

5. Cultivating Resilience: Resilient organizations are created by capable leaders who cultivate an environment that values flexibility, creativity, and ongoing development. They promote candid dialogue, teamwork, and education, enabling staff members to offer suggestions, resolve issues, and assist one another in times of need.

Decision-Making Processes in Times of Uncertainty

1. Evaluating the Circumstance: Accurate and thorough situation assessment is the first step in making decisions during emergencies. To do this, pertinent data must be gathered, data must be analyzed, and the nature, extent, and effects of the crisis on the organization and its stakeholders must be understood.

2. Determining Priorities and Objectives: Leaders need to decide on strategic goals and priorities for response and recovery actions after the situation has been evaluated. These could include goals for maintaining operations, serving customers, managing reputation, keeping employees safe, and maintaining financial stability.

3.   Evaluating Options: Leaders must consider a variety of options and alternatives when making decisions when the situation is uncertain in order to address the crisis. In order to make an informed decision, this may entail weighing the possible risks and benefits of different courses of action and consulting advisors, stakeholders, and subject matter experts.

4. Weighing Benefits and Risks: Leaders have to weigh the possible advantages and disadvantages of every choice they make, balancing short- and long-term effects with strategic priorities. To make sure that choices are in line with the organization's beliefs, objectives, and interests, this calls for thorough investigation, critical thinking, and judgment.

5. Consulting Stakeholders: To get feedback, obtain perspective, and forge agreement on important choices, decision-making during crises frequently entails consulting with stakeholders. To get input, address issues, and increase support for suggested actions, this may entail interacting with staff members, clients, vendors, government organizations, and members of the local community.

6. Taking Determined Action: Leaders need to take decisive action during uncertain times in order to put plans and decisions into action that effectively handle the crisis. This calls for the guts, assurance, and conviction to take calculated chances and make difficult decisions in the face of uncertainty and complexity.

7. Monitoring and Adjusting: Making decisions during emergencies is a process that must be continuously observed, assessed, and adjusted. Leaders have to monitor how decisions are being implemented, evaluate how they are affecting the situation, and adjust as needed in response to evolving risks, new information, and changing conditions.

To sum up, effective crisis management relies heavily on decision-making and leadership to steer organizations through difficult times and guarantee successful crises responses. Setting the tone, giving direction, making difficult choices, communicating clearly, and fostering resilience within the company are all characteristics of effective leaders. In uncertain times, decision-making calls for a number of steps, including situation assessment, goal and priority identification, option evaluation, risk and benefit analysis, stakeholder consultation, decisive action, monitoring, and necessary adjustments. Through effective crisis management and wise decision-making, organizations can successfully navigate difficult times and come out stronger on the other side.

Chapter 5: Building Resilience

Building resilience is crucial for organizations to survive and bounce back from shocks, adjust to changes, and prosper in a fast-paced, unpredictable world. We will look at methods in this part for strengthening organizational resilience and developing a resilient culture inside the company.

Strategies for Building Organizational Resilience

1. Identification and Evaluation of Risks: Identifying and evaluating potential risks and vulnerabilities that could affect the organization's operations, reputation, and stakeholders is the first stage in developing organizational resilience. This entails carrying out in-depth risk assessments, reviewing previous information, and projecting potential dangers to the company.

2. Contingency and Scenario Planning: Planning scenarios entails imagining possible future events and creating plans of action and backup plans to deal with them. Organizations can improve their preparedness and reactivity to unforeseen events by modeling various crisis scenarios

and creating reaction strategies for each one.

3. Redundancy and Diversification: Spreading risks throughout several product categories, markets, business lines, and geographical areas helps diversify an organization and lessen its reliance on any one revenue stream or risk exposure. Building backup systems, resources, and procedures is known as redundancy, and it guarantees that activities will continue even in the case of disruptions.

4. Adaptability and Flexibility: To effectively respond to evolving threats and changing situations, organizations must be flexible and adaptable. This entails creating an environment where workers are inspired to

take advantage of growth opportunities and adjust to new difficulties through innovation, experimentation, and continual improvement.

5. Collaboration and Partnerships: By utilizing shared resources, expertise, and networks to address shared challenges and accomplish mutual goals, collaboration and partnerships with external stakeholders, such as suppliers, customers, government agencies, and community organizations, can improve organizational resilience.

6. Infrastructure and Technology Investment: Building organizational resilience requires investments in infrastructure and technology that allow businesses to take use of digital tools and

platforms for data analytics, communication, and remote work. Building resilience requires a strong IT infrastructure, cybersecurity precautions, and disaster recovery strategies.

7. Training and Development of Employees: Employee development and training programs are essential for fostering organizational resilience because they give staff members the abilities, information, and skills they need to handle emergencies and adjust to shifting circumstances. This covers instruction in decision-making, communication, crisis management, and emergency response.

Cultivating a Resilient Culture within the Organization

1. Leadership Commitment: Leadership commitment and support are the first steps in creating a resilient culture. Leaders need to show that they are dedicated to fostering resilience, explain to staff members the value of resilience, and set an example for others by embracing change, overcoming obstacles, and growing from failures.

2. Transparency and Open Communication: Fostering a resilient culture where employees feel empowered to share ideas, voice concerns, and work together to find solutions requires open communication and openness. It is imperative for leaders to

promote candid communication, pay attention to input from staff members, and be upfront and honest about the objectives, difficulties, and tactics of the company.

3. Autonomy and Empowerment: Giving workers autonomy and decision-making ability empowers people to accept responsibility for their work, make wise choices, and adjust swiftly to changing conditions. Leaders should assign tasks, offer resources and assistance, and have faith in their staff members to make significant contributions to initiatives aimed at fostering resilience.

4. Education and Adjustment: Building resilience inside the organization requires fostering a culture of learning and

adaptation. This entails promoting experimentation, accepting failure as a teaching tool, and persistently looking for input and new ideas to enhance procedures, frameworks, and tactics.

5. Training and Development for Resilience: Employees' resilience skills and capabilities can be improved by offering them opportunities for resilience training and development.

Training on stress management, emotional intelligence, problem-solving, and resilience-building methods may be part of this to assist staff members in overcoming hardship and succeeding in trying circumstances.

6. Recognition and Reward: Giving resilience behaviors and contributions credit strengthens their significance and motivates staff members to keep exhibiting resilience at work. Leaders should recognize and reward resilience wins, whether they involve conquering challenges, coming up with novel solutions, or helping out colleagues in trying times.

7. Work-Life Balance Promotion: Supporting employee resilience and well-being requires promoting work-life balance. It is imperative for leaders to motivate their staff to prioritise self-care, establish clear boundaries, and seek assistance when required to sustain their mental, emotional, and physical well-being outside of the workplace.

To sum up, in today's dynamic and complicated business climate, businesses must develop a resilient culture and build organizational resilience in order to overcome obstacles, navigate uncertainty, and prosper.

Organizations can improve their capacity to endure crises, adjust to change, and come out stronger on the other side by putting resilience building strategies into practice, such as risk identification and assessment, scenario planning, adaptability, collaboration, and investment in employee training and development. Leadership commitment, open communication, empowerment, learning, acknowledgment, and work-life balance promotion are all necessary to cultivate a resilient culture that fosters an environment that is both supportive and adaptable, allowing people to flourish and make valuable contributions to the success of the company.

Chapter 6: Innovation and Adaptation

Effective crisis management requires both adaptation and innovation in order for companies to adjust to changing conditions, overcome obstacles, and take advantage of growth and improvement opportunities. This part will look at ways to use technology and creativity for adaptation, as well as the significance of embracing change and innovation in times of crisis.

Embracing Innovation and Change in Times of Crisis

1.   Opportunity Amidst Adversity: Organizations frequently have the chance to innovate and adjust to new circumstances during crises. Organizations can not only weather crises but also prosper in the long run by embracing change and looking for creative answers to new problems. This necessitates a mental adjustment from seeing crises as exclusively bad things to seeing them as opportunities for change and development.

2. Agility and Flexibility: In order to react swiftly to shifting conditions and new opportunities, adaptation and innovation

require agility and flexibility. To effectively overcome uncertainty, organizations must be prepared to modify their tactics, reassess their presumptions, and try out novel ways. To concentrate on areas with the biggest impact, this may entail reorganizing operations, reordering projects, and reallocating resources.

3. Risk-Taking and Trying New Things: As firms journey into unfamiliar areas to explore new ideas and solutions, innovation inevitably requires risk-taking and experimenting. In order to spur innovation and ongoing development, leaders must promote an environment of experimentation during times of crisis. This involves giving staff members the freedom

to take measured risks, learn from mistakes, and refine their ideas.

4.   Customer-Centricity: Customers' requirements, preferences, and behaviors are frequently altered by crises, necessitating that businesses modify their offerings in terms of goods, services, and experiences. Organizations can spot chances for innovation and provide value-added solutions that cater to changing customer demands and preferences by keeping a close eye on customer feedback, trends, and insights.

5. Adaptability and Resilience: Because companies need to be able to foresee changes in their external environment and respond to them effectively, adaptation and

innovation are intimately related to organizational resilience and adaptability. Organizations can position themselves for long-term success and sustainability by proactively identifying and addressing emerging challenges and opportunities by cultivating a culture of resilience and adaptation.

Leveraging Technology and Creativity for Adaptation

1. Making Use of Digital Transformation: Technology is essential for facilitating innovation and adaptation in times of crisis because it gives organizations the means to interact, cooperate, and function from a distance. Cloud computing, artificial

intelligence, and data analytics are a few examples of digital transformation projects that can improve an organization's agility, efficiency, and resilience. This will help the firm take advantage of new possibilities and quickly adjust to changing conditions.

2. Encouraging Collaboration and Remote Work: Employees may work and collaborate efficiently from any location with the help of remote work and collaboration solutions, which promote flexibility and creativity. Teams can remain in touch, share ideas, and work together on projects in real time, no matter where they are physically located, thanks to virtual communication platforms, project management tools, and collaboration software.

3.   Encouraging   Creativity   and Experimentation: Since creativity helps companies come up with new ideas and solutions to challenging issues, it is crucial for fostering innovation and adaptability. Leaders need to foster a creative culture where staff members are free to question the status quo, think creatively, and try out novel ways to problem-solving.

4.   Encouraging   Interdepartmental Cooperation: Cross-functional collaboration is often the catalyst for innovation, as different viewpoints and specialties combine to address difficult problems. By dismantling departmental silos, promoting multidisciplinary teams, and cultivating a collaborative and knowledge-sharing culture across departments and disciplines,

organizations can help promote cross-functional collaboration.

5. Encouraging Staff Innovation: Since frontline staff members are frequently in the best position to spot opportunities for innovation and improvement in their day-to-day work, employee creativity is a potent driver of organizational adaptability and innovation. It is recommended that organizations enable their workforce to provide innovative ideas, insights, and proposals by establishing avenues for feedback, acknowledgment, and assistance for efforts spearheaded by employees.

6. Investing in Innovation and R&D Labs: Organizations can foster experimentation, creativity, and innovation through research

and development (R&D) projects and innovation laboratories. Organizations may investigate novel technologies, test novel concepts, and create prototype solutions in a controlled setting before expanding them for wider use by investing in R&D and innovation laboratories.

To sum up, in times of uncertainty and crisis, an organization's ability to adapt and innovate is essential to its success. Organizations can effectively handle crises, embrace chances for development and progress, and emerge stronger on the other side by embracing change, cultivating an innovative culture, and utilizing technology and creativity for adaptation. By encouraging agility, flexibility, risk-taking, and experimentation as well as giving staff members the freedom to share their ideas and insights in order to further organizational performance, leaders can play a critical role in fostering adaptability and innovation. Organizations must prioritize adaptation and innovation as fundamental capabilities in order to stay competitive, resilient, and future-ready in a business environment that is changing quickly as the pace of change quickens and crises become more complicated.

Chapter 7: Recovery and Lessons Learned

The process of managing a crisis involves recovery and lessons gained, which help organisations overcome difficulties, resume operations, and strengthen their resilience going forward. This section will look at ways to recover and restore after a disaster and how organisations may use the lessons they learn to become more resilient in the future.

Steps for Recovery and Restoration Post-Crisis

1. Evaluation and Assessment: Undertaking a thorough assessment and review of the crisis's effects on the organization's operations, stakeholders, and resources is the first step in the recovery process. To do this, information must be gathered, the degree of the damage must be assessed, and areas that need to be addressed right away must be identified.

2. Maintenance and Stabilization: After the assessment is finished, the emphasis switches to situation stabilization and maintaining vital operations. To handle urgent needs and restore critical services, this may entail mobilising resources, putting in place temporary fixes, and turning on backup systems.

3. Interaction with Stakeholders and Communication: In order to keep stakeholders aware of the organization's intentions, activities, and progress, communication is essential during the recovery period. Timely and transparent communication shows the organization's dedication to accountability and openness while also assisting in the restoration of stakeholder trust and confidence.

4. Resource Allocation and Prioritisation: In order to properly address urgent demands and resume operations, recovery efforts frequently necessitate rigorous resource allocation and prioritization. Prioritizing initiatives according to their impact, viability, and alignment with strategic objectives is imperative for organizations to

ensure that scarce resources are directed towards the areas where they may yield the greatest impact.

5. Rebuilding and Restoring: Rebuilding damaged infrastructure, fixing systems and procedures, and getting operations back to pre-crisis levels are all part of the reconstruction and restoration phase. Coordinating with vendors, contractors, and other parties may be necessary to speed repairs and guarantee a prompt return to routine.

6. Observation and Adjustment: Organisations have to keep a close eye on things during the recovery process, assess what's working and adjust tactics as necessary. This calls for adaptability and

agility to deal with shifting conditions, new difficulties, and crisis-related lessons.

7. Review and Assessment: Organisations should carry out a comprehensive assessment and analysis of their response activities to pinpoint their advantages, disadvantages, and opportunities for development when the recovery is finished. This include determining if reaction tactics are effective, assessing the effect on stakeholders, and recording lessons gained for future use.

Learning from Crises to Improve Future Resilience

1. Root Cause Analysis: The first step in learning from crises is to identify the underlying causes of the crisis by performing a root cause analysis. In order to identify areas for improvement, this entails looking at the order of events, spotting weaknesses and vulnerabilities in systems and procedures, and evaluating response and decision-making processes.

2. Identifying Lessons Learned: Lessons from the crisis should be identified by organisations, taking into account both achievements and failures as well as areas for improvement. This could entail gathering feedback from important stakeholders, carrying out post-mortem analyses, and recording best practices and suggestions for later use.

3. Modifying Guidelines and Protocols: To improve future resilience, organisational policies, processes, and protocols should be updated based on lessons learnt from disasters. This could entail upgrading risk assessments, updating crisis management plans, and adding fresh perspectives and suggestions to normal operating procedures.

4. Development and Training: Employees can gain important knowledge, skills, and talents from crises that will help them respond to challenges in the future. In order to help employees grow from their past experiences, improve their resilience, and get ready for future crises, organisations should offer training and development opportunities.

5. Establishing an Educational Culture: Developing a culture of learning is crucial to utilising the knowledge gained from disasters to increase resilience in the future. To create organisational success, organisations should cultivate a culture that values and rewards ongoing learning, introspection, and improvement. This will enable staff members to provide their thoughts and insights.

6. Sharing Best Practices: Enhancing collective resilience and readiness can be achieved by disseminating best practices and crisis-learned lessons to other organisations, industry partners, and stakeholders. This could entail taking part in networks, conferences, and forums within the industry where businesses can share

information, work together to find solutions, and gain insight from one another's experiences.

7. Creativity and Ongoing Improvement: Crises frequently inspire creativity and innovation in organizations as they look for novel approaches to deal with obstacles and adjust to change. Companies should promote an innovative and continuous improvement culture where staff members are free to try out novel concepts, question the status quo, and effectuate constructive change.

In summary, recovery and lessons gained are crucial elements of the crisis management process that help organisations overcome hardship, draw lessons from the past, and strengthen their resilience going forward. Organisations can rebuild infrastructure, stabilise operations, and win back stakeholder confidence by adhering to post-crisis recovery and restoration procedures.

Conducting root cause analysis, identifying lessons learned, updating policies and procedures, offering opportunities for training and development, creating a culture of learning, exchanging best practices, encouraging innovation and continuous improvement are all part of learning from crises and enhancing future resilience. Leveraging lessons learned from crises can help organisations emerge stronger, more adaptable, and better equipped to confront opportunities and challenges in the future as they continue to navigate uncertain and demanding circumstances.

Chapter 8: Case Studies and Best Practices

Analysing actual crisis management situations can give organisations important insights into the approaches, manoeuvres, and best practices they can use to overcome obstacles and come out on top. In order to identify best practices and lessons from effective crisis responses, we will examine case studies of significant crisis management incidents in this section.

Case Study: Johnson & Johnson Tylenol Poisoning Crisis (1982)

The 1982 Tylenol poisoning incident that Johnson & Johnson encountered is among the most well-known instances of successful crisis management. After consuming Tylenol capsules laced with cyanide, seven people in the Chicago area passed away. Many people look to Johnson & Johnson as a role model for crisis management because of their prompt and decisive response to the crisis.

Key Lessons Learned:

1. Prioritising Public Safety First: Even though it would have cost a lot of money,

Johnson & Johnson immediately put public safety first by pulling 31 million bottles of Tylenol capsules off store shelves nationwide. This preventative action served to show the company's dedication to customer safety and shielded customers from future harm.

2. Ethical Communication: Throughout the crisis, the company kept lines of communication open and transparent with the public, the media, and governmental organisations. James Burke, CEO of Johnson & Johnson, regularly addressed the media, gave timely updates on the situation, and discussed the recall and the investigation. Building credibility and trust with stakeholders was facilitated by this open and honest communication.

3. Cooperation with Authorities: To find the source of the contamination and guarantee the security of its products, Johnson & Johnson worked closely with the FDA, law enforcement, and other regulatory organisations. The company exhibited its dedication to regulatory adherence and public health by cooperating with authorities.

4. Rebuilding Customer Trust: Johnson & Johnson put their products in tamper-resistant packaging after the crisis, which included introducing triple-sealed tamper-evident caps. Through these actions, consumers' trust in the Tylenol brand was restored and they were reassured about the integrity and safety of the product line.

Case Study: Airbnb's Response to COVID-19 Pandemic

The COVID-19 pandemic of 2020 presented hitherto unseen difficulties for the travel and hospitality sector, requiring businesses such as Airbnb to quickly adjust to evolving conditions and lessen the effects on their operations and stakeholders.

Key Lessons Learned:

1. Adaptability and Flexibility: By swiftly altering its business strategy to accommodate shifting client demands and preferences, Airbnb showed flexibility and adaptability. Aware of changing consumer needs and safety concerns, the company

launched new programmes and features including online experiences and improved cleaning procedures.

2. Supporting Guests and Hosts: During the pandemic, Airbnb put financial aid programmes, enhanced safety measures, and cancellation policies first in order to support its hosts and guests. The company offered refunds and travel credits to guests affected by travel restrictions, and it provided financial relief to hosts affected by cancellations.

3. Social Engagement: Airbnb gathered input, addressed issues, and worked together to find solutions from its community of hosts, guests, and local stakeholders. The company started a

number of community-supporting programmes, including giving frontline employees free or discounted lodging and virtual experiences to help hosts and amuse visitors during lockdowns.

4. Openness and Communication: Regarding the pandemic's effects on its operations, business, and response efforts, Airbnb kept its stakeholders informed in an honest and open manner. In order to keep hosts, guests, and staff members informed of the most recent advancements and initiatives, the company regularly updated its website, blog posts, and social media channels.

Best Practices and Lessons Learned:

1. Eager Planning and Readiness: Establishing clear roles, responsibilities, and protocols for response and recovery, as well as creating comprehensive crisis management plans and performing risk assessments, are all proactive ways that organisations can plan and get ready for crises.

2. Putting the safety and wellbeing of stakeholders first: During times of crisis, organisations have an obligation to put the safety and well-being of their stakeholders—employees, clients, suppliers, and the community—first. Implementing safety precautions, offering assistance and support, and being open and honest about risks and safety measures are some examples of how to do this.

3. Efficient Interaction and Openness: During times of crisis, maintaining credibility and fostering trust with stakeholders requires open and prompt communication. In order to provide accurate information and promptly address concerns, organisations should communicate openly about the situation, response efforts, and plans.

4. Collaboration and Partnerships: The process of enhancing crisis response and recovery efforts can be facilitated by collaboration and partnerships with external stakeholders, such as government agencies, industry partners, and community organisations. To coordinate resources, exchange information, and work together on

solutions, organisations should take advantage of their current networks and relationships.

5. Learning from Disasters: Organisations can identify their strengths, weaknesses, and opportunities for improvement in their crisis management capabilities by using the valuable learning opportunities that crises present. Post-crisis evaluations should be carried out by organisations, and they should record lessons learned and integrate input into future planning and readiness initiatives.

Conclusively, case studies showcasing successful crisis management incidents offer significant perspectives on the approaches, manoeuvres, and optimal techniques that institutions can employ to effectively handle obstacles and emerge more resilient from hardship. Organisations can strengthen their resilience, adaptability, and readiness to meet upcoming opportunities and challenges by putting stakeholder safety first, communicating clearly, working with partners, and learning from crises. Organisations that want to stay competitive, resilient, and prepared for the future must adapt and innovate their crisis management strategy as the complexity of crises rises and change happens at a faster rate.

Chapter 9: Future Trends and Challenges

In order to effectively handle crises and preserve resilience, organisations need to keep ahead of emerging trends and foresee future issues as the business landscape changes and gets more complicated. We will look at new developments in crisis management in this area, as well as potential opportunities and problems in an unpredictable environment that is always changing.

Emerging Trends in Crisis Management

1. Digital Transformation: The continuous digital transformation is changing how organisations handle crises by allowing them to use data analytics and technology to prepare, respond, and recover more effectively. Digital solutions like social media monitoring apps, crisis communication platforms, and predictive analytics are quickly becoming vital parts of crisis management plans.

2. Virtual Collaboration and Remote Work: Organisations are having to adjust to managing crises in a dispersed and decentralised environment, which is having an impact on crisis management

procedures. This is due to the trend towards remote work and virtual collaboration. Coordination of crisis response operations and preservation of business continuity are becoming more and more dependent on online collaboration tools, virtual communication platforms, and distant incident response teams.

3. Globalisation and the Sturdiness of Supply Chains: Global supply chains are becoming more integrated, which offers crisis managers both benefits and challenges. Natural catastrophes, geopolitical unrest, and pandemics are examples of risks that organisations must foresee and reduce in order to prevent supply chain disruptions. They must also strengthen their resilience by implementing

strategies like redundancy, diversification, and strategic partnerships.

4. Cybersecurity Threats: The surge in cyberthreats, encompassing ransomware assaults, compromised data, and cyberespionage, presents noteworthy obstacles for crisis management practitioners. To handle increasing cyber threats and vulnerabilities, organisations need to bolster their cybersecurity posture, put in place strong incident response strategies, and work with industry partners and government agencies.

5. Climate Change and Sustainability: As organisations deal with the effects of extreme weather events, natural disasters, and environmental crises, climate change

and environmental sustainability are becoming more and more important factors in crisis management strategies. Organisations looking to reduce environmental hazards and increase long-term resilience are increasingly prioritising sustainable business practices, resilience planning, and community involvement.

Anticipated Challenges and Opportunities

1. Intricacy and Unpredictability: Crisis management faces tremendous obstacles due to the business environment's growing complexity and unpredictability. Organisations have to balance competing agendas and stakeholder interests while

navigating a wide range of linked risks, such as geopolitical instability, technology innovation, regulatory changes, and public health catastrophes.

2. Misinformation and Information Overload: The abundance of data and the dissemination of false information on social media pose difficulties for decision-making and communication during times of crisis.

To combat false information and uphold credibility, organisations need to sort through enormous volumes of data, evaluate the veracity and correctness of the information, and interact with stakeholders in an efficient manner.

3.   Adaptability and Resilience: Organisations constantly struggle with developing resilience and adaptability, which calls for a proactive, all-encompassing approach to risk management and readiness. To effectively handle changing threats and challenges, organisations need to regularly review and update their crisis management strategies, make training and development investments, and cultivate a culture of creativity and resilience.

4. Compliance with Law and Regulation: Crisis management is made more difficult by the need to adhere to legal and regulatory duties, especially in highly regulated sectors like healthcare, finance, and energy. During times of crisis, organisations have to strike a balance between adhering to the law and

ethical, operational, and reputational issues, as well as industry norms.

5. Reputational Risk Management: With the potential to have long-term effects on stakeholder trust, brand equity, and consumer loyalty, safeguarding and strengthening an organization's reputation is a vital task during times of crisis.

To reduce negative effects on their reputation and business performance, organisations must proactively manage reputational risks through efficient communication, open decision-making, and prompt issue resolution.

Opportunities for Innovation and Growth

1. Decision Making Based on Data: Organisations can improve their crisis management capabilities by using data-driven decision-making, thanks to the growing availability of data and analytics. Organisations can anticipate possible effects, discover new hazards, and improve reaction plans to reduce risks and increase resilience by utilising data analytics, predictive modelling, and machine learning algorithms.

2. Collaboration and Partnership: Organisations can improve their crisis management skills by collaborating and forming partnerships with other

stakeholders, such as governmental bodies, trade groups, educational institutions, and non-profits. Organisations can improve mutual goals, coordinate response activities, and strengthen collective resilience by exchanging information, resources, and knowledge.

3. Innovation in Technology and Tools: Organisations can improve their crisis management skills by utilising innovations in technology and tools like blockchain, Internet of Things (IoT), and artificial intelligence. Organisations can enhance situational awareness, automate repetitive operations, and enable real-time communication and cooperation in times of crisis by utilising developing technology.

4. Sturdy Supply Chains: Establishing robust and sustainable supply chains offers organisations the chance to reduce risks and improve their ability to withstand disruptions. Organisations can lessen their reliance on a single source of supply, lessen their susceptibility to interruptions, and add value along the entire supply chain by diversifying their suppliers, putting strong risk management procedures in place, and adopting the concepts of the circular economy.

5. Enhanced Involvement with Stakeholders: Increasing stakeholder involvement and communication gives organisations a chance to become more credible, trustworthy, and resilient in times of crisis. Organisations may improve their

reputation, fortify their resilience against upcoming difficulties, and fortify their relationships with stakeholders by cultivating an open dialogue, soliciting feedback from stakeholders, and exhibiting empathy and transparency.

In summary, companies looking to improve their preparedness and resilience in an unpredictable environment face both possibilities and threats from emerging trends and problems in crisis management.

Organisations may enhance their crisis management capabilities, effectively navigate crises, and emerge from adversity stronger and more resilient by embracing new trends, addressing expected problems, and grabbing chances for innovation and growth. For long-term success and sustainability, proactive and strategic approaches to crisis management will be crucial as organisations continue to adapt and change in response to shifting opportunities and threats.

Conclusion

To sum up, crisis management is a complex field that calls for early preparation, clear communication, and quick decision-making in order to overcome obstacles and remain resilient in the face of uncertainty. We have examined several facets of readiness, reaction, recuperation, and adaptability during this investigation of crisis management techniques, gaining knowledge from actual case studies, industry best practices, and developing trends.

Understanding the nature of crises and its possible effects on communities, stakeholders, and organisations is the first step towards effective crisis management. Organisations may enhance their ability to anticipate and mitigate risks, minimise disruptions, and safeguard the well-being of their stakeholders by doing comprehensive risk assessments, creating strong crisis management strategies, and establishing well-defined processes for reaction and recovery.

In times of uncertainty, communication is essential to crisis management because it helps organisations establish credibility, trust, and openness with stakeholders. Organisations can mobilise resources, coordinate emergency activities, and aid in recovery and restoration when they communicate transparently and promptly. They also reassure stakeholders and build trust.

Effective crisis management also requires strong leadership, as these individuals are responsible for offering their colleagues direction, counsel, and support in times of need. Leaders may create confidence, foster a sense of purpose, and enable staff members to contribute their thoughts and efforts to the organization's reaction and recovery activities by exhibiting empathy, resilience, and decisiveness.

Moreover, organisations must learn from crises in order to strengthen their resilience and get ready for new challenges.

Organisations can adapt to changing conditions and overcome adversity by strengthening their crisis management capabilities, performing post-crisis reviews, identifying lessons learnt, and adopting corrective actions and enhancements.

Emerging trends, opportunities, and problems, including digital transformation, remote work, cybersecurity concerns, sustainability, and climate change, will define crisis management in the future. To improve their resilience and readiness in a changing and uncertain environment, organisations need to keep ahead of these trends, foresee future difficulties, and take advantage of growth and innovation opportunities.

In summary, crisis management is a continuous process that necessitates continuing assessment, modification, and enhancement in order to successfully traverse obstacles and preserve resilience in a world that is constantly changing. Organisations may improve their capacity to handle crises, safeguard their stakeholders, and prosper in the face of uncertainty by adopting proactive planning, good communication, strong leadership, and a dedication to learning and innovation.